Sacred & Satiric

Medieval stone carving in the West Country

JH BETTEY
and
CWG TAYLOR

REDCLIFFE
Bristol

First published in 1982 by
Redcliffe Press Ltd, 14 Dowry Square, Bristol 8

To Judith,
who has been a constant source of help
and without whose enthusiasm the
project would not have been completed

ISBN 0 905459 32 6

Typeset and printed in Great Britain by
Penwell Ltd, Parkwood, Callington, Cornwall

Contents

The illustration depicts a ninth century cross-shaft from Codford St. Peter near Warminster. This shows a Spring fertility dance, and is possibly intended to represent the Celtic god Sucellos, a god of fertility and plenty who was often shown as a dancing man with a mallet in his hand and holding aloft a branch or foliage.

Acknowledgements

We acknowledge with thanks the help of the clergy of the various churches for their assistance in taking the photographs and for permission to publish them.

Introduction

The medieval churches of the West Country contain many thousands of stone carvings, and this wealth of medieval art is only a small fragment of what once existed before the destruction of the sixteenth and seventeenth centuries and the over-zealous restorations of the Victorian period. The carvings themselves range from the crudely executed work of unskilled country masons to the most skilful and elegant medieval workmanship; and their subject matter includes deeply religious themes, scenes from the life of Christ, Our Lady and the Saints, as well as monsters, grotesques, fertility figures, pagan symbols and coarse satires on everyday life. There is also much elaborate carving of foliage and other decoration on capitals, niches for saints, corbels, roofs, window tracery, towers and wall surfaces. Many of the best preserved and most interesting of these carvings are difficult or even impossible to appreciate from ground level. Some are high up on towers or parapets; others take the form of corbels or roof bosses of which the naked eye can see little detail. Only with the help of the modern long-focus lens can the full splendour and interest of these carvings be revealed.

This study illustrates just a few of the many figure carvings which are to be found on parish churches, cathedrals and former abbeys in an area of some 30 or 40 miles around Bristol, in the county of Avon and parts of Gloucestershire, Wiltshire and Somerset. The task of selecting the illustrations out of all the carvings in the region has been very difficult. The aim has been to illustrate not just the well-known sculptures such as those at Wells, Malmesbury or Bristol, but also to show something of the rich and varied carvings which may be found in parish churches throughout the region. The figure-carvings discussed and illustrated here are found either on the church buildings themselves or on such essential features as pillars, fonts, screens and roof bosses; the carvings on tombs and sepulchral monuments and memorial effigies are a separate subject and are not included.

During the Middle Ages the Bristol area possessed in abundance the two essential pre-requisites for producing good stone carvings: one was the easy availability of several different sorts of easily carved good quality stone, the other was a large number of wealthy and pious patrons who were ready to lavish money on the adornment of their churches. This book will consider first the different sorts of stone which were used; next the patrons such as the great religious houses, the guilds and societies, the parish churches, and the many wealthy laymen and groups of humbler parishioners all of whom helped to pay for the work of the carvers; the subjects portrayed by the carvers, their developing styles and the work which survives will be discussed; and finally the extent of the losses which occurred at the Reformation and during the changes in religious attitudes during the sixteenth and seventeenth centuries will be summarised.

1 *The Stone*

Within or near the Bristol area lie many of the best stone quarries of medieval England, especially quarries producing fine and varied limestones. The stone from these quarries has been used in parish churches, cathedrals, monasteries, country houses and cottages throughout the area, and adds immeasurably to its charm and character; the same stone has also been used to produce the varied carvings in local churches. There were numerous local quarries which supplied stone to their immediate neighbourhoods, and one of the delights of a journey through any part of the region is to see how the stone used in churches and secular buildings, walls and hedges changes every few miles and to observe the subtle differences in the qualities, colours and textures of the various stones. Among the most notable quarries were those of Dundry Hill whose stone has been so important in the buildings of Bristol and was used on the Augustinian abbey church which was later to become Bristol Cathedral, on St Mary Redcliffe and on many of the other parish churches which were so numerous in the medieval port of Bristol. The excellence of Dundry stone can also be appreciated in the tower of Dundry itself, high on its hillside overlooking Bristol and in the magnificent church of Yatton on the flat lands between Bristol and Weston-super-Mare. A multitude of quarries to the east of Bath produced oolite stone which was extensively used during the Middle Ages. Much of the finest stone came from Hazelbury quarry near Box, and it was this stone which was used in the abbey churches and buildings at Malmesbury,Stanley, Bradenstoke and Lacock, and some of the finest surviving medieval sculpture in the region including the superb south doorway of Malmesbury Abbey and the roof bosses in the cloisters at Lacock are of this stone. Stone from the Box quarries was also used for many of the parish churches and manor houses of north and west Wiltshire. In the south of Wiltshire the most important quarries were at Chilmark and Tisbury, producing a fine quality oolite, creamy white when it comes from the quarry and assuming a characteristic greenish tinge when exposed to the weather. From the Chilmark quarries came the stone for Salisbury Cathedral, for the medieval castle at Wardour and for a host of parish churches throughout that district. In east Somerset the finest stone came from the quarries at Doulting near Shepton Mallet. This is the grey-coloured stone of which much of Wells Cathedral and Glastonbury Abbey were built and which is to be found in numerous parish churches in that area, including the towers at Chewton Mendip, Leigh-on-Mendip, Batcombe and Evercreech, with their fine figure-carving. In south Somerset the incomparably beautiful honey-coloured stone from Ham Hill was available. For many people this is the most attractive of all English stones, and its use was widespread in churches and houses throughout south Somerset and west Dorset, and it is to be found in the superb towers and fine carvings of such churches as

Kingsbury Episcopi, Ile Abbots, Ilminster and Sherborne as well as in those most attractive of English houses Montacute, Barrington, Melbury, Lytes Cary, Chantmarle, Brympton D'Evercy, and in numerous others in that district. The easily carved stone from Ham Hill was also popular with medieval sculptors throughout the region.

North of Bristol, the cream coloured or pale golden stone of the Cotswolds was used. This stone came from a multitude of small quarries situated all along the Cotswold escarpment, so that almost every village had its own quarry from which came the material for its parish church as well as for the houses of the parishioners. It is this uniformity of source as well as the natural attraction of the stone that gives so much charm to places such as Castle Combe, Biddestone, Painswick, Tetbury, Fairford and many others. The following pages will also show some of the fine medieval carving for which this stone has been used. Not only was the Bristol area well supplied with abundant stone of high quality and attractiveness, but equally important for the carver was the fact that these finely-grained oolites were very easy to work and comparatively soft when first they came from the quarry. It was this which made possible such a wealth of finely-executed and highly detailed work.

2 *The Stone-Carvers' Patrons*

As well as good quality stone, the Bristol area was also rich in patrons for the medieval builders and stone-carvers. It was a wealthy area, especially during the later Middle Ages when the wool and cloth trade brought so much prosperity; it was also well supplied with rich monastic houses, with wealthy, pious laymen and with parish guilds and societies which vied with each other in lavishing money on enlarging, beautifying and adorning their parish churches. The results of their piety and of their rivalry can be clearly seen in the churches, which are often far larger than was necessary to accommodate the medieval inhabitants of each parish, with their lofty and elaborate towers built at enormous expense, and with a wealth of surviving stone carving. Many of the great monastic churches have gone or survive only in fragments. The greatest and wealthiest of them all, the monastery at Glastonbury, exists now only as a ruin, while many others have vanished completely like the former great churches at Muchelney, Cleeve, Keynsham, Stanley and Bradenstoke, or the great Benedictine nunnery at Shaftesbury, once the richest nunnery in England. Enough carving survives however at, for example, Malmesbury and Lacock, in the former Augustinian abbey church at Bristol now the Cathedral, in the ruins at Glastonbury, in the former Augustinian priory church at Leonard Stanley or in the church of the former Benedictine abbey at Sherborne, to show what a wealth in stone carving, as in so much else of great beauty was lost at the Reformation and to emphasise the importance of the monastic houses as patrons of the arts. Some of the larger churches such as the cathedrals at Wells and Salisbury or the monasteries at Glastonbury and Malmesbury, maintained a permanent staff of masons and stone carvers, whose influence can be discerned in the parish churches for many miles around. These great churches, in touch with the most advanced styles of architecture, design, carving and workmanship had a profound effect upon the parish churches of the area, providing a standard in architecture and also no doubt in liturgy, furnishing and decoration.

For a few parish churches there is documentary evidence to show how the addition of an aisle or a tower or the provision of a statue or other carving was paid for by a single individual. All such documentary evidence comes from the end of the Middle Ages, and we have little indication of how the money was obtained to pay for earlier enlargements, rebuildings or for carvings and other decorations. At North Cadbury the whole church was rebuilt during the early fifteenth century at the expense of Lady Elizabeth de Botreaux who intended to establish a college of priests there; the Hungerford family was responsible for rebuilding the church at Wellow during the same period. At High Ham documentary evidence survives to show how the whole of the nave and chancel were rebuilt in 1476 at the expense of a few wealthy parishioners and local gentlemen led by Abbot John Selwood of Glastonbury. The main body of the church with its finely carved tracery and large gargoyles is all said to have been completed within the one year, 1476. The last abbots of Glastonbury lavished money not only on their own abbey but also on local parish churches, and the initials 'J.S.' for John Selwood (Abbot of Glastonbury 1456-92) can be found on a bench-end at East Brent, and 'R.B.' standing for Richard Bere (Abbot 1493-1524) are prominently displayed on the porch at Chedzoy and may also be found at Bruton, Othery and Westonzoyland. At Mells the richly carved and sumptuously decorated church was rebuilt during the early sixteenth century and the money was raised by the parishioners; John Leland in c.1540 commented that it was built 'yn tyme of mynde . . . by the hole paroche'. The remarkable polygonal two-storeyed chapel on the south side was, however, the gift of a London draper named Garlande and was built about 1485. In Wiltshire the highly ornate south aisle at Bromham known as the Tocotes and Beauchamp chapel, with its elegant late medieval stonework and fine figure carving, was built at the expense of the two families during the 1490s. The rebuilding of the great Gloucestershire churches of Chipping Camden, Fairford and Northleach was paid for by the wealthy wool-merchants the Grevels, the Tames and the Forteys respectively, and there are many other similar though less ostentatious examples. In Bristol the rebuilding of St Mary Redcliffe is forever associated with the name of William Canynges although other merchants were also involved; the fine tower of St Stephen's with its delicately carved tracery, was paid for by the merchant John Shipward who was mayor of Bristol; a large part of St John's church was paid for by Walter Frampton, a merchant who died in

1388, while on Dundry Hill overlooking the port of Bristol the elegant landmark of the church tower was paid for in 1484 by the Merchant Venturers of Bristol. The church at Great Chalfield was built at the expense of the Tropnell family; the north aisle at Steeple Ashton was paid for by the Long family, the south aisle by the Lucas family, both wealthy wool and cloth merchants. The relationship between wealth and wool is made clear at Seend near Devizes where the ornate north aisle of the nave was built by a clothier John Stokes who died in 1498 and where the window jamb above the brass memorial to Stokes and his wife is decorated both inside and out with clothiers' shears. John Cantelow, the prior of Bath, gave an east window to the nearby church of St Catherines; and Peter Carslegh the vicar of Winscombe in Somerset, gave a window to the church there depicting three different saints who bore his name, Peter.

But the majority of parish churches had no single wealthy benefactor, and depended entirely on the efforts of the whole body of parishioners for any extensions or additions to the fabric or for the commissioning of carvings. Evidence of the way in which this was done, and of the tremendous enthusiasm which the parishioners as a body showed towards the enlarging and adornment of their parish churches survives in the form of late medieval churchwardens' accounts, wills, bishops' licences and other documentary material. From this evidence it is possible to see more precisely how images and other stone carvings were acquired for the churches. At Yatton, for example, the splendid series of late medieval churchwardens' accounts shows how the whole parish combined to raise money for their church, and how this money was spent on various projects including the purchase of 69 images for the rood screen. The Yatton accounts show payments for the purchase of stone and lime, for the payment of masons and carvers, for the building of a parapet around the roof of the church with numerous figures carved upon it, and for an elaborately carved churchyard cross. At Chewton Mendip the evidence of wills shows how money was being left during the first half of the sixteenth century to complete the magnificent tower there with its finely carved figure of the Risen Christ surrounded by angels carrying instruments of the passion. At Croscombe near Shepton Mallet the churchwardens' accounts survive for the fifteenth century and show the way in which the inhabitants combined to beautify their parish church. There were several guilds or societies devoted to raising money for the church and one of their projects was the purchase of a fine stone statue of St George for one of the side chapels. In 1508 the statue was ordered from a stone carver in Exeter called John Carter and more than £27 was spent on 'The Jorge', and on transporting it to Croscombe and on its painting and decoration. Although the statue of St George at Croscombe was destroyed during the Reformation, some evidence of the enthusiasm of the medieval parishioners for beautifying their church can still be seen, for the Treasury with its strongly barred windows in which the money they raised was kept and where the church plate and other valuable possessions were stored, survives on the south-west side of Croscombe church.

Even more detailed evidence concerning the purchase of a carving and showing the sort of rivalry that existed between neighbouring congregations in the decoration of their churches, comes from the church of St James in Bristol. The contract survives, made by the churchwardens on behalf of the parishioners, with two carvers Richard and Roger Ridge of Staffordshire, for the carving of a highly elaborate and ornamented reredos for the high altar in 1498. The work was to cost £110 and it was specified that it was to be as good as or better than the reredos at the nearby Bristol church of St Stephen. The new reredos was to be intricately carved, brightly coloured and was to contain a large number of images of the saints. A few years later, in 1505, a further large addition was made to the furnishings of St James, when Roger Ridge of Staffordshire was commissioned to make two screens of the same standard of work as the reredos ('as workmanly made'), with an Easter Sepulchre and numerous decorations including 'xiiii pendaunt Angells on the xiiii postes there beyng now in the Roof of the same'; the new work was to cost £43. The surviving late medieval records of other Bristol churches show the way in which carvers were employed to provide costly additions to their furnishings. Inventories of church goods also show how the parish churches of the region on the eve of the Reformation were full of statues and other carvings as well as of colour, lights, jewels, vestments, manuscript books and other precious things, most of which vanished or were destroyed a few years later during the Reformation changes. At Pilton between Glastonbury and Shepton Mallet, for example, an inventory of 1508 lists silver crosses, chalices, candlesticks and plate, seventeen different suits of vestments and hangings for the altars and no less than thirty-three kerchiefs to cover the various statues in the church during Lent. The church at Beckington had statues of the Virgin, St John the Baptist, St John the Evangelist, St George, St Christopher, the Trinity and St Osyth. An inventory of the goods of St Ewen's church in Bristol made in 1455 shows the magnificence of the interior and the number of stone carvings and images in the church. There was a high altar with a carved reredos of Derbyshire alabaster and gilded images of the Blessed Virgin and the twelve apostles. Lights were maintained before the statue of St Ewen, the patron saint, and before several other statues, and other carvings which are mentioned include St John, St Catherine, St Margaret, the Evangelists, the Patriarchs and 'our Lord in our Lady's armes'. The churchwardens' accounts of St Nicholas in Bristol for 1468 show that the church had just acquired a new reredos for the High Altar, with carved figures of the Holy Trinity, the Blessed Virgin, St Nicholas and St Blaise. Even after the first changes of the Reformation the parishioners of St Nicholas continued to lavish money on their church, and in 1542 John Naylard a stone-carver was paid 8s. 0d. 'for makyng of the Imagys of Adam and Eve and the angell and a mytyre for a Image of Synt Clement'. At All Saints' in Bristol during the early sixteenth century twenty-two carved stone images of saints are mentioned, while at St Mary Redcliffe during the fifteenth century William Canynges gave to the church an Easter Sepulchre elaborately carved with images of saints and angels and 'Hell made of timber and ironwork thereto, with Divels to the number of 13'.

3 *The Carvers*

Turning to the men who produced the carvings for the medieval churches, we know disappointingly little about any of them; nor do we have much more information about most of the builders, masons, carpenters and other craftsmen employed in building the churches. One persistent myth can be disposed of at the outset; the work was not done by monks, but by professional craftsmen and tradesmen employed sometimes by monasteries or cathedrals, sometimes by the churchwardens of parish churches, and at other times employed upon secular buildings. Chance references in contracts and account rolls have preserved the names of a few of the masons and carvers, but beyond this, information about the men themselves is very difficult to find. During the Saxon and early medieval period stone carving was not a separate function but was merely one of the masons' tasks, since carvings were generally an integral part of the building in which they were employed. Thus carvings were to be found as part of the structure of doorways or capitals, corbels or label-stops, and were fashioned by the same men who made the arches and the tracery. The Romanesque carvings on doorways, capitals, vaults and windows as at Malmesbury, Leonard Stanley, Elkstone, Compton Martin or Bristol Cathedral were an integral part of the structure, not a separate, later addition. Even the corbel tables around the eaves of so many Norman churches as at Elkstone and Lullington, or the tympana as at Moreton Valence, Quenington, Siston and elsewhere, are essentially a part of the building and not merely a decorative addition. Only slowly during the thirteenth century did a separate group of 'imagers' grow up as the demand increased for free-standing statues, effigies, images and other carvings and as the fashion for realism developed. During the fourteenth century groups of specialist carvers began to be assembled at certain quarries such as those at Corfe Castle in the isle of Purbeck who produced the Purbeck stone or 'marble' fonts, tombs, effigies, pillars and decorative columns for dispatch all over England. At the Ham Hill quarries masons and carvers produced the standardised pillars and capitals, windows and doors of Ham stone which are to be found over wide areas of south Somerset and west Dorset. Many of the fine carvings and statues as well as window tracery, capitals, mouldings and doorways may indeed have been carved at workshops some distance away from the churches for which they were intended. Some of the great abbeys and cathedrals such as Malmesbury and Wells could of course provide employment for specialised stone-carvers for long periods. The great west front at Wells obviously provided work for carvers as well as masons for many years. Occasionally it is obvious from the style of a carving in a parish church that it was created by a craftsman from a local abbey. A good example is at Lullington near Frome, where an exceedingly elegant statue of Christ in Majesty over the north doorway which has been dated to c.1170 is obviously from the same workshop as that producing the figure carving all over the south porch at Malmesbury, and the nave clerestory there which has the same characteristic decorative roundels that surround the figure of Christ at Lullington. Similarly the fine Norman carving of the seated Christ with his feet on a dragon which is on the west wall of Stanton St Quinton obviously came from the nearby workshop at Malmesbury. John Stowell, freemason, of Wells who was working on Wells cathedral throughout the 1460s, was employed by the nearby parish church of St Cuthbert in 1471 to carve a stone reredos for an altar in the south aisle. Part of this reredos, the subject of which was the Tree of Jesse, still exists, although in a badly mutilated form.

Parish churches did not always confine themselves to local carvers or to nearby workshops when ordering statues. The examples of a statue for Croscombe being ordered from Exeter and of a reredos of St James' Bristol being ordered from Staffordshire have already been quoted. In the latter case the reason for going so far was probably to obtain work in Derbyshire alabaster which had become such a popular material for carvings during the fifteenth century. Another example of a parish commissioning work from a distant carver occurs in the Pilton churchwardens' accounts for 1523. With both Wells and Glastonbury near at hand, the churchwardens might have been expected to go to a workman there for a stone-carved image. Instead we find the entry '. . . for my expense to Exsetter to speke with ye carver 2s. 4d.' Contracts for carvings and other building work occasionally mention other churches which were to be used as models, and show that the sources of inspiration were by no means always local, even when the work was ordered by parishioners themselves. The churchwardens at Yatton went to various neighbouring churches and to Bristol to look at screens before ordering one for their own church in 1446; while carved work at St James, Bristol ordered in 1498 was to be like that in nearby St Stephen's. But when the churchwardens of Banwell ordered a new screen in 1519 they specified that it should be like that recently constructed at St Erth in Cornwall, and men were sent from Banwell to St Erth to view the screen and were given 4d. 'for paper to draw the draft of ye rode loft'. It cost 8s. 4d. to draw up the agreement with the carver, and the total cost of the screen came to nearly £40.

Although a few of the surviving contracts specify some of the details of the work to be done, it is clear from others that considerable latitude was allowed to the carver as to the subject-matter and style of many of the minor carvings or as to the details of carved work on capitals mouldings, the bases for statues and much exterior work. This point will be discussed presently in connection with the secular, pagan and even coarse carvings which are not uncommon in churches, but here the point can be illustrated from two surviving contracts for towers. In 1372 Nicholas Wyshongre or Wishanger made a contract with the churchwardens and parishioners of Arlingham in Gloucestershire to build a tower for their parish church. Few details were laid down except that the tower was to be built over three years, there was to be a handsome west window (*'una fenestra artificialiter constructa inter primum fundum et secundum'*), and small windows in each face of the tower at the uppermost storey. The top of the tower was to be finished with battlements, and the mason was to set corbels inside the tower to carry the various floors. But details of carving, finishing, tracery and decoration are clearly left to the mason to complete in a workmanlike manner and are not laid down precisely in the contract. Likewise in 1442 the churchwardens and parishioners of Dunster made a contract with John Marys, a mason from nearby Stogursey, for a central tower to their parish church. The contract stipulated that the tower was to be 100 feet in height, and that it was to be paid for at the rate of 13s. 4d. per foot, the parishioners supplying all the materials. The windows in the tower were to be made according to the pattern or design of Richard Pope a free mason who was at that time engaged in work on Sherborne Abbey ('according to the patron ymade by the advyce of Rychard Pope Fremason'). But apart from this, very few conditions about the manner in which the tower was to be constructed were laid down in the contract, except that it was to be built 'after reason and good proportion', a phrase which obviously left the mason with a good deal of freedom. The battlements of the tower were to be made 'suffycyantly', and three gargoyles were to be made at the three corners of the tower ('Allso the sayde Jon Maryce schall make iii gargylles in three corners of the sayde towre'); the fourth corner was occupied by the stair turret. But again there is no mention of the form that the gargoyles should take and it must presumably have been left to the inventive imagination of John Marys what hideous monsters or fearful demons he chose to carve as decorative finishes to the water spouts. Another interesting point which emerges from the Dunster contract is that few men were employed in building the tower and there was very little mechanical assistance. Consequently it was stipulated in the contract that if any of the stones were so large that John Marys and his two or three workmen could not lift them, then the parishioners were to provide additional muscle-power:

> *'Allso if there be any stone y-wroughte of such quantity that ii men or iii at moste may not kary (carry) hym, the sayde parishe shall helpe hym'.*

The two main tools used by medieval masons and carvers were the axe and the chisel. The rough work of dressing stones was obviously done with the axe, and the tooling marks made by axes can still be seen on countless stones in medieval churches, diagonal marks on flat surfaces and vertical on rounded surfaces such as pillars and the mouldings of doorways. The mason's axe can be seen being used in many medieval illustrations, an instrument with two blades or faces, one like an axe proper, the other a sharp hammer head. The handle was made of ash. With this tool the medieval craftsmen could produce shaped stones, smooth-faced and squared, and could also execute remarkably intricate mouldings and shapes, and it is probable that much Saxon carving was done entirely with the axe. For the intricate work of carving and for finishing, the chisel was used, and the sophisticated, elaborate carvings of the Gothic period were clearly the work of the chisel.

From the surviving contracts, churchwardens' accounts and other incidental references we do know the names of several late medieval carvers who worked in the region, but we know very little about the men themselves or their careers. Geoffrey Kerver of Worcester was paid £13 6s. 8d. in 1463 for work and carving at All Saints' Church, Bristol; John Norton, a mason of Bristol, was in charge of work at St Mary Redcliffe when William Worcestre visited the church in 1480 and recorded its dimensions. The carvers Richard and Roger Rydge of Staffordshire who worked on St James' Bristol during the late Middle Ages have already been mentioned, as has also John Marys of Stogursey who built the central tower at Dunster in 1442. William Hort 'free mason' was paid more than £9 in 1525 for his work on the elaborately carved churchyard cross at Yatton; John Carter 'free mason of Exeter' built the north-eastern chapel of St George at Croscombe between 1506 and 1512 at a cost of £27 11s. 8d., and was also paid for carving a large statue of the saint for the new chapel, 'the wardens Owyn Porter and Edward Bolle hath y payd owtte of the box of the cherch money £1 10s. 0d. unto John Carter the Jorge maker at the settyng oppe of the Jorge (i.e. image of St George)'. Apart from these and several other similar references, however, we know little of the carvers, and of those who did most of the carving or of the building work in our parish churches we know nothing. But it is clear that apart from major statues and schemes such as those at the great cathedrals and abbeys, or specialised work such as roof bosses, many of the smaller carvings and carved decorations on the parish churches was done by masons like John Marys of Stogursey who were not specialists and who combined carving and building work on churches with a variety of other work on secular buildings.

Once the carvings were installed in a church, the work on them was not finished, for churchwardens' accounts and the evidence of the surviving carvings make it clear that most of them were painted and gilded. The comparatively colourless interiors of our churches would have been quite alien to the feelings of the Middle Ages, and the walls were covered with colourful paintings, such as those which can still be seen so splendidly at Kempley in Gloucestershire and in a few other places, the woodwork of screens and roofs was painted, like the restored example of the roof of St Cuthberts, Wells, and the statues were likewise adorned with colour. Almost as much was often paid for painting the sculpture as was spent upon its carving. The churchwardens' accounts of Yatton, for example, have abundant evidence of this love of expensive colouring: in 1512 the Yatton churchwardens paid John Walelyn the large sum of £19 10s. 0d. 'for peynting and gylding of ye church', and in 1529 they made the following payments:

'payd for gylting of Saynt James 13s. 5d.
payd for gylting of owre Lady 6s. 0d.'

It is clear from these and many other accounts that images, capitals, wall surfaces, tombs and even some of the external carvings such as those on churchyard crosses were liberally covered with paint and gilding. The lapse of centuries together with the efforts of Victorian restorers have so effectively removed much of this colour that it now requires a considerable leap of the imagination to recreate in the mind's eye the colourful and even garish appearance which the interior of medieval churches must have presented. Medieval churchgoers delighted in colour and it was spread upon all possible surfaces, both within and outside the churches. We can only dimly conceive of what the effect of this must have been, and of the startling impact which for example the west front of Wells must have had when the statues were decorated in rich blues and greens, reds and yellows. The modern admiration for the texture of bare stonework would have been quite strange to medieval congregations.

4 *The Subjects of the Carvings*

The subject matter of the figure sculpture which survives in churches clearly divides into two sections: the religious and sacred subjects such as aspects of the life of Christ, the Blessed Virgin and the Saints; and the secular, pagan or even profane carvings which appear in such profusion. One of the fascinations of medieval churches is to see how again and again the sacred and the profane are to be found side by side, how religious subjects are intermixed with blatantly pagan fertility symbols, and with an assortment of demons, devils, grotesques, monsters and obscene creatures as well as with carvings which evidently represent the coarse humour of medieval masons. We have always to remember that it was the sacred and religious carvings which provoked the wrath of sixteenth and seventeenth century reformers, and that large numbers of carvings which the Puritans regarded as superstitious or idolatrous have been defaced and mutilated or have disappeared entirely, while the secular subjects often escaped such destruction. We have also to remember that many carvings, especially those on roof bosses or high up on towers are not easily visible from the ground and were not therefore so readily apparent to medieval congregations as they are to us with the help of the modern long-focus lens. Nonetheless this mixture and juxtaposition of the sacred and the secular, the religious and the profane, is still a remarkable feature of our churches.

In spite of all the efforts of puritan reformers and Victorian restorers, the contrasting subjects bear striking witness to the continuing influence of older cults upon the minds of medieval parishioners and masons, and to the persistence of the idea of the conflict between good and evil which so powerfully occupied the minds of church carvers throughout the Middle Ages.

The Religious Subjects

The earliest churches of the area were the 'minsters' from which priests made preaching journeys into the surrounding pagan countryside to teach, to celebrate mass and to baptise converts. The memory of these Saxon minsters survives in numerous place-names; it also survives in the fragments of Saxon carving to be found in many churches of the region. Often these carvings were part of elaborately decorated Saxon crosses, or cross-shafts which perhaps marked the sacred sites even before the building of the churches. Remnants of such crosses can be seen at Bibury and Somerford Keynes in Gloucestershire, at Colerne and Ramsbury in Wiltshire, at Kelston in Avon and at Nunney, Rowberrow and West Camel in Somerset. One of the most impressive surviving Saxon cross fragments is at Melbury Bubb in north Dorset where the circular stone was later turned upside down and made into a font, but where the typical Saxon carving—wild, frantic interlaced patterns, and entwined animals—can still clearly be seen. The role of the Saxon churches in bearing witness to the Christian faith in a dark world was no doubt a major reason why the tradition developed of prominently displaying the 'Rood', the figure of the crucified Christ, on Saxon churches. Remains of such roods, or evidence that they once existed can be seen at several west-country Saxon churches, notably at Bitton in Avon, Daglingworth and Deerhurst in Gloucestershire, Langford just over the border in Oxfordshire, Romsey and Headbourne Worthy in Hampshire, and Bradford-on-Avon in Wiltshire. At Bradford-on-Avon two large angels, each about five feet long, face each other high up on the east wall of the nave. These no doubt formed the supports to a much more elaborate composition, probably of a crucifixion such as those which survive from the Saxon period at Romsey in Hampshire and Daglingworth in Gloucestershire. The carved figures of Saxon angels which survive at Deerhurst in Gloucestershire and Winterbourne Steepleton in Dorset also once formed part of such roods.

The church which provides the most striking evidence of its origin as a missionary centre, and which also reveals something of the fervour and enthusiasm which must have inspired the early Christian missionaries is at Breamore in Hampshire, a few miles down the Avon from Salisbury. Here much of the structure of the church survives intact from the 10th century; a Saxon arch inside the church has deeply cut above it the Anglo-Saxon inscription HER SPVELAD SEO GECWYDRAEDNES DE—'In this place the Word is revealed unto thee'. Above the entrance to the church at Breamore is the Saxon rood, the figure of the crucified Christ, not in repose as at Daglingworth, Langford or Romsey, but with body twisted in the agony of the crucifixion, a work of art which still possesses a powerfully moving force in spite of the mutilation which it received at the hands of reformers during the sixteenth century. Similarly, on the southern face of the tower at Beverston in Gloucestershire is a defaced but still remarkably powerful pre-Conquest carving of the Risen Christ holding a tall cross.

Other Saxon and early Norman religious carvings which survive in the Bristol area include the lovely Virgin and Child from Inglesham in north Wiltshire. This delightful composition shows the Virgin holding the figure of Christ, depicted not as a baby, but as a little boy holding in his hand a book, while above can be seen the hand of God. Another early carving of the Virgin and Child can be found above the chancel arch in the delightful little church of Langridge near Bath. A fine Norman carving of the triumphantly risen Christ seated in Judgement can be seen in the *tympanum*, or space filling the archway above the door, at Elkstone between Cheltenham and Cirencester. Here Christ in Majesty is surrounded by the symbols of the Evangelists, (the angel of St Matthew, the lion of St Mark, the ox of St Luke and the eagle of St John), and by the Agnus Dei, while above is the hand of God: around are biting beaks, human heads and grotesque ornaments. This tympanum is not very skilful in design, nor is it particularly well carved, but the whole creates a charming composition. Similarly attractive and vigorous though unsophisticated carvings are found on the two tympana at Quenington to the east of Cirencester. One subject is the Coronation of the Virgin; in a somewhat crowded composition, Christ and his Mother sit side by side surrounded by the symbols of the Evangelists, and beside them a little domed temple, perhaps intended to represent the heavenly mansions. The other Norman tympanum at Quenington depicts the Harrowing of Hell, the apocryphal story of how after his crucifixion Christ descended into Hell and preached to the spirits of the damned, saving some who clung to his Cross. At Quenington, Christ is shown forcing open the jaws of Hell to pluck forth the souls with his Cross, while behind him is the sun, 'the Dayspring from on high' piercing the darkness of sin. Again this is a naive carving, clearly not the work of a great master, but nonetheless remarkably moving in the simplicity and vigour of its style, the triumphantly risen Christ dominating and subduing the powers of darkness, while the sun is shown with a little human face. A much more sophisticated Norman carving of the Harrowing of Hell is to be seen at Bristol cathedral, and there is another at South Cerney. The great black stone carving of the Harrowing of Hell in Bristol cathedral, seven feet high, and remarkably powerful, is one of the most important works of art in the area which survive from the pre-Conquest period. The figure of Christ stands out from the deeply cut background dominating the jaws of Hell and reaching downwards with his cross to snatch up two tortured souls from the abyss. The whole composition is an excellent example of the skill and inventiveness of the late Saxon carvers, and again reminds us of how much has been lost by the work of iconoclasts in the sixteenth century.

Other Saxon and Norman religious carvings include the Agnus Dei, the Lamb bearing the cross and banner of the Resurrection, which can be seen on tympana at Stoke-sub-Hamdon and Langport, and the Tree of Life, a piece of originally oriental and pagan symbolism which enjoyed a great popularity among early Christian carvers, being taken to represent the tree of Man's fall in the Garden of Eden and the Cross of Man's Redemption by Christ; this appears on the Norman tympana at Siston, Stoke-sub-Hamdon, and, elaborately carved with beasts and framed by biting heads, at Lullington near Frome. The figure of Christ above the north door at Lullington is set between decorative discs or *paterae*, identical to those on the south wall of the nave at Malmesbury, and the Lullington figure together with the ornate doorway beneath was obviously produced by a carver from Malmesbury, and perhaps was actually carved in the workshop there.

Undoubtedly the most popular theme for Saxon and Norman carvers was that of the conflict between the forces of good and evil and of the necessity for the protection of the Church and its sacraments if the assaults of the devil and his hosts upon the individual soul were to be resisted. This sense of the protection afforded by the Church to the otherwise helpless soul, and of the incessant conflict with the powers of darkness, is seen in many Norman carvings of the battle between St Michael the Archangel and the devil or the dragon representing the power of evil in the world. Such conflicts are to be seen on the north wall of Stoke-sub-Hamdon, above the south door at Flax Bourton, on the fine Saxon font at Avebury in Wiltshire and the notable Norman font at Luppit just over the Somerset border in Devon, and on the fine font at Locking near Weston-Super-Mare, in the powerful tympana at Moreton Valence in Gloucestershire depicting a vigorous battle between St Michael and the Dragon, or in the primitive Norman carving over the doorway at Ampney St Mary near Cirencester which shows the Lion of Righteousness triumphing over the snake-like dragon of Evil. In a powerful Norman carving at Stanton St Quinton in Wiltshire the figure of the seated Christ is shown with his feet resting on and subduing the dragon.

A similar conflict between the Virtues and their contrary Vices is depicted on the Norman fonts at Stanton Fitzwarren in Wiltshire and Southrop in Gloucestershire. At Stanton Fitzwarren the Virtues—*Largitas, Humilitas, Pietas, Misericordia, Modestia, Temperencia, Paciencia* and *Pudicicia*—are shown trampling enthusiastically upon their corresponding Vices—*Avaricia, Superbia, Discordia, Invidia, Ebrietas, Luxuria, Ira* and *Libido*. At Southrop the figures of the Vices each have their names carved backwards in 'mirror' writing on the panels as a further indication of their wickedness, while around the top of the font, above the conflict, are depicted the heavenly mansions to which the soul may aspire by holding fast to the Virtues through the help of the Church, and eschewing the Vices and all the works of the Devil.

The Saxon font at Avebury shows in symbolic form the powers of evil which are cast out by the sacrament of Baptism, while the font at Rendcomb is guarded by the Norman figures of eleven of the apostles with an uncarved space in the place for Judas. The ornate Norman font at Lullington near Frome is even more explicit concerning the essential protection against evil afforded by the Church and its sacraments, for deeply-cut around the rim of the font is the Latin inscription: *Hoc fontis sacro pereunt delicta lavacro* ('By the washing in this holy font sins perish'). During the later medieval centuries the same sort of imagery, designed to convey an identical message, occurs in the paintings with which the walls of many churches were so lavishly decorated, in the stained glass windows, and in the illustrations of the 'Doom' or Last Judgement which were so frequently to be found in churches and of which a magnificent example survives in the great west window of Fairford, or above the chancel arch at St Thomas's, Salisbury. The most dramatic, unified composition which survives in the Bristol area from the Norman period, is undoubtedly the great south porch at Malmesbury Abbey, which is one of the finest pieces of Norman sculpture in the whole country. The carvings date from c1150-1170, and although some of the figures are badly weathered and defaced, it is still possible to recognise the extent of the ambitious project. The outer doorway has scenes from the Old and New Testaments, the Creation, the Story of Man, the Fall, the Old Testament figures, the Birth and Life of Christ, the Passion, Crucifixion and Resurrection. Within the porch on either side, huge tympana display the seated figures of the Apostles, and the smaller inner tympanum shows Christ in Majesty. The fine design and workmanship as well as the ambitious concept of this remarkable porch at Malmesbury represent a great advance on anything that had previously been seen in the west country, and can only be equalled in expansive design by the great west front at Wells which was not built until a century later.

Scenes from the life of Christ between the Nativity and the Passion are rare. A carved capital in the Norman church of Leonard Stanley illustrates the gospel story of the woman washing Christ's feet and drying them with her hair; and a series of fifteen roof bosses in the nave at Tewkesbury depicts various incidents from the life of Christ. The comparative neglect of the biblical stories relating to the life of our Lord and of the Old Testament stories of the Creation, the Fall, Noah, Moses and the prophets is remarkable, especially as these figure largely in illuminated manuscripts and in the surviving fragments of stained glass, and are shown superbly in the two fine collections of stained glass which survive in west-country parish churches, at Fairford in Gloucestershire and St Neot in Cornwall. The exceptions to this are the ambitious scheme around the south porch of Malmesbury Abbey, and the incomparable west front at Wells, the richest collection of thirteenth century sculpture anywhere in England. The construction of the west front of Wells marks the full emergence of English Gothic sculpture. The scheme was complex and ambitious, involving 176 full-length statues, 30 half length angels, and 134 smaller reliefs, 85 panels depicting the Resurrection, and in the centre the Virgin and Child, the Coronation of the Virgin and Christ in Judgement, flanked by archangels and apostles, the whole front of the cathedral being used as a framework for the vast design. The statues themselves were originally richly coloured, crimsons, greens, reds and yellows, and must have presented a spectacle that to modern eyes would have seemed garish, certainly startling and perhaps even vulgar. The work was done between 1220 and 1260. The basic scheme underlying the complex series of statues and carvings at Wells was the complete story of Man from the Fall to the Redemption, and includes the principal figures and scenes from the Old Testament, with the patriarchs and prophets, the life of Christ, the apostles, evangelists, saints and the theologians, the patrons and benefactors of the English church, and the final Resurrection with naked figures emerging from their graves at the Day of Judgement. Above the main door is successively the Virgin and Child, the Coronation of the Virgin and, towering over the whole composition, Christ in Majesty. The complex and magnificent design of this vast composition on the west front at Wells must have been the work of a learned theologian, skilled in iconography and open to influences from abroad and aware of contemporary developments in church building and decoration in Paris, Rheims and Amiens. Perhaps it was the great Bishop Joscelin who was Bishop of Bath and Wells during the years 1206-1242, but there is no surviving evidence to establish the facts. The statues themselves were probably worked in the quarries at Doulting and brought ready-finished to Wells, and for such an enormous work a large number of craftsmen must have been employed over many years, and indeed there are considerable differences in the size and workmanship of individual statues. The detailed, scholarly theme and the quality of the workmanship in these Doulting-stone carvings, is an eloquent tribute to the skill of the masons and carvers of the sculptural school at Wells during the thirteenth century.

From the thirteenth century to the Reformation, the religious subjects portrayed by the stone-carvers grew more numerous and, in many churches, much more sophisticated. It will be convenient here to deal in turn with some of the main subjects found in the Bristol area. The figures of the Trinity or of the Father and the Son are to be found at several places. This is represented for example on the opulent west front at Yatton by the figure of God the Father, with the crucified Christ between his knees, and the subject also appears on the tower at East Brent. The Persons of the Trinity are shown in three roof bosses in the south transept of St Mary Redcliffe; they are shown as heads, God the Father as an aged man, Christ shown unmistakeably wearing the Crown of Thorns and with both hands raised to show the wounds; the Holy Ghost is shown as an old man with long hair and a beard. Hidden in the hair and beard of the Holy Ghost, and quite impossible to see from the floor of the church without powerful optical aid are various animal and human heads including one grotesque. Why they should be there is a great mystery. Is there some hidden symbolism, were they a mischievous addition by the carver, or merely an indication of his fertile imagination and fantasy? Such puzzles, like many other features of medieval art, still defy interpretation.

The figure of the Risen Christ is depicted in many carvings. Two almost identical representations are to be found on the western faces of the late medieval towers at Batcombe and Chewton Mendip in Somerset. Although the towers themselves are quite different in style and appearance, the carvings must have been the work of the same carvers or school of carvers. Both show the figure of Christ surrounded by angels bearing the Instruments of the Passion. At Batcombe the angels are depicted with feathered legs appearing beneath their flowing draperies, possibly a reflection of the fact that the only angels the carver had seen were the actors in mystery plays whose costumes may well have included feathered coverings for the legs. The fact that different stone carvers probably used some common source, possibly a drawing or illustration from an illuminated manuscript, for their inspiration, can be seen in the similarity of treatment which the Resurrection is given in numerous carvings both in stone and wood. Almost identical carvings of the triumphant Christ coming forth from the tomb and of the sleeping soldiers who had been set to guard it occur on the tower at Ile Abbots, on a roof boss in St Mary Redcliffe and on wooden bench ends at Hatch Beauchamp and Bishops Hull near Taunton. On a roof boss at Steeple Ashton Christ is shown surrounded by Prophets and Sybils, while the figure of Christ in Glory on a roof boss at Wells cathedral is attended by angels. A figure of Christ on a roof boss in the choir of Gloucester cathedral is surrounded by angels carrying musical instruments, while another figure of Christ in Glory survives from the fifteenth century at Croscombe in Somerset, and there is a fine early sixteenth century representation of the crucifixion at Rendcomb.

The Instruments of the Passion were a particularly popular subject with west-country carvers both in wood and stone. Many examples survive on wooden bench ends, and they are to be seen on stone roof bosses at St Mary Redcliffe and Malmesbury, while at Lacock parish church as in several other churches angels are shown carrying the Instruments. The subject is also depicted in medieval stained glass at Leigh-on-Mendip.

A remarkably interesting statue of Christ is on the tower at Fairford. The statue which is about four feet high is an example of the 'Image of Pity' or 'Christ in Pity' which became very popular during the later Middle Ages, since prayers addressed through it were popularly credited with great efficacy. The Risen Christ is depicted still wearing the Crown of Thorns and carrying the Resurrection Cross, his right hand is raised in blessing, while the spear wound in his side is visible. Especially interesting is the fact that the statue appears to be much earlier than the late medieval church at Fairford. In fact the statue is probably contemporary with the church which was largely rebuilt by the Tame family soon after 1490, but the style is a deliberate attempt to revert to and copy the Romanesque tradition of three or four centuries earlier. The details of the figure of Christ, who is shown naked except for a drapery around his loins, are treated in the flat fashion of a much earlier period, and the whole appearance of the figure is quite different from that of late Gothic sculpture. Nevertheless this is a fine, forceful carving, and an extremely attractive, sensitive work of art.

The Blessed Virgin was especially popular as an intermediary during the later Middle Ages, and although statues of the Virgin roused the violent antagonism of sixteenth century iconoclasts and very large numbers were destroyed, many remain, often in inaccessible positions, and they can be found on churches all over the region. Carvings of the Virgin and of her emblem the lily are to be found for example on the towers at Banwell, Brislington and East Brent, and on roof bosses at St Mary Redcliffe where there is an Annunciation, a Virgin and Child and a Coronation of the Virgin, at Steeple Ashton where there is an Assumption of the Virgin, at Bishopstone near Salisbury, Lacock, on the abbey ruins at Glastonbury, on the font at Crowcombe which shows the Virgin with her mother St Anne, and in many other places.

Other religious subjects can be dealt with very briefly. Apostles and saints are frequently to be found on roof bosses, for example at Bristol Cathedral, St Mary Redcliffe and the former nunnery at Lacock. A sadly mutilated Tree of Jesse survives at St Cuthberts in Wells as the reredos to an altar in the south aisle. It was made in 1471 by a local mason John Stowell, and the original contract for the work survives; Stowell was no doubt a member of the remarkable school of carvers working at Wells during the later Middle Ages, using Doulting stone, and finding most of their work in the cathedral and in the production of tombs and monuments. The Jesse reredos at St Cuthberts consisted of a representation of the geneaology of Christ through the family of Jesse, a subject which is still to be found in several surviving stained glass windows, and most notably in the tracery of the great Jesse window at Dorchester Abbey in Oxfordshire. At Wells the reclining figure of Jesse can still be discerned and fragments of the heads and bodies of his descendants as well as the foliage of the 'Tree' can still be seen, showing that the original must have been a finely constructed and colourful composition, but all was sadly defaced at the time of the Reformation and provides only an inkling of the high quality of the sculpture. As will be shown later, such attacks upon what they regarded as idolatry have denuded the churches of the region of much of their finest sculpture. One place where most of the original statues survive is at Ile Abbots in south Somerset. Here the charming remote church has one of the finest towers in Somerset. Built of the golden stone of Ham Hill, it retains no fewer than ten of its original statues in the niches around the tower, and although these are not of the highest quality of medieval workmanship and have in any case weathered considerably after five centuries of exposure to Somerset rain, wind and frost, nonetheless they do show the remarkable range of saints represented on the tower of a quite ordinary parish church, and serve to remind us of how much sculpture was lost from inside and outside parish churches at the time of the Reformation. The Ile Abbots statues consist of the Blessed Virgin, the Resurrection, St Peter and St Paul on the western face of the tower; John the Baptist with the Agnus Dei in his hand, and St Clement with a papal tiara, the double cross and anchor on the eastern face; on the south side St Margaret, St Katherine and St George; and on the north the Archangel Michael.

Secular and Profane Subjects

In marked contrast to the comparatively small number of religious subjects, the profusion of subject-matter depicted in non-religious carvings seems almost limitless. It remains a matter for speculation why it was that from the earliest Saxon church buildings to the elegant and sophisticated edifices built at the very end of the Middle Ages, it seemed good to the builders to decorate their churches with monsters, grotesque objects and mythical creatures, and, more remarkably still, to include among the carvings so many symbols of pre-Christian religious and fertility cults.

The traditional view that the grotesque forms and horrid monsters shown on the outside of churches illustrate merely a warning against the dreadful demons that lie in wait for the Christian soul once it leaves the security of the church is no doubt greatly over-simplified, since such monsters are to be found carved within as well as outside the buildings. But they may very well represent one side of the continuing conflict between good and evil which so powerfully occupied the minds of the earliest iconographers. This however does not explain the presence of so many pagan and frankly sensual subjects, nor does it adequately account for the survival of pre-Christian religious symbols which are to be found carved on so many churches. The view that these also represent warnings against vice, and against the lusts of the flesh which would inevitably lead the Christian soul to perdition, seems simplistic and unsatisfactory. It certainly does not account, for example, for the tremendous popularity of the Green Man or Jack o' the Green, for carvers in both wood and stone, nor for the way in which this pre-Christian symbol of vegetative fertility is to be found both inside and outside churches throughout the region, from Norman town churches like St John's, Devizes in Wiltshire, or in remote situations like Broomfield in Somerset, to sophisticated, late medieval churches like St Mary Redcliffe or parts of the Cathedral in Bristol, or Wells Cathedral and Bishops Lydeard in Somerset. The most probable explanation for the continuing popularity of this piece of symbolism, or of the obviously pagan male and female fertility figures, serpents, dragons and severed heads, as well as for Roman carvings and altar stones incorporated into several churches, would seem rather to lie in the way in which the early Christian church deliberately absorbed the pagan customs and traditions rather than attempting totally to destroy them. That this was clearly conscious policy of the early church in England is shown by a famous letter written by Pope Gregory to Abbot Mellitus in AD 601, in which the Pope declared that he had given much thought to the conversion of the English and advised that the pagan temples should not be destroyed, but rather purified with holy water and Christian altars set up within them instead of the idols. In surroundings which already had powerful and familiar religious associations the people would be won more easily to the new faith. Thus many Christian churches throughout the region were built on sites of obvious religious significance in pre-Christian times. For example, the church at Knowlton in Dorset is situated inside a Neolithic henge monument in the centre of the ceremonial circle, and the churches at Stanton Drew in Avon and Avebury in Wiltshire are beside the standing stones of the remarkable prehistoric monuments there, the church on the hill-top at Oldbury on Severn which is of Saxon origin and is dedicated to a Saxon saint, St Arilda, is situated inside a circular prehistoric earthwork which was probably also a pre-Christian religious site. In the same way as the church absorbed various pagan festivals into its own feasts like Christmas and Easter, and substituted its own celebrations in place of pagan saturnalia, so pre-Christian symbols continued to decorate the walls of Christian churches.

It is necessary also to take into account the fatalistic beliefs generally current throughout the Middle Ages, and later, and to remember that there co-existed with Christianity a powerful sub-culture of belief in witchcraft, magic and fertility cults and in the powers of evil. It is also important to remember the power of conservatism in medieval life. The fact that 'time out of mind' it had been the accepted custom to decorate the churches with monsters, grotesques and pagan symbols as well as with the figures of Christ and His saints would have provided a powerful incentive for continuing to do so. Finally the availability of high-quality local stone, the skill and exuberance of local stone carvers and the local rivalry between parishes in the extension, decoration and adornment of their churches, all provided a powerful impetus for the practice to continue throughout the Middle Ages and afterwards. During the nineteenth century the revival of interest in medieval architecture and decoration, and the construction of pseudo-Gothic churches, revived also the idea of decorating the exteriors with beasts, monsters and gargoyles as well as with figures of the saints.

It is not only to the twentieth century mind, however, that the practice of including secular and profane carvings on the walls of churches seems odd. St Bernard, in the twelfth century, reproached his fellow monks because of the pagan symbols with which they adorned even the monastic churches and cloisters, and was as puzzled as we are to know what purpose they were intended to serve:

> '. . . what profit is there in those ridiculous monsters, in that marvellous and deformed comeliness, that comely deformity? To what purpose are those unclean apes, those fierce lions, those monstrous centaurs, those half-men, those striped tigers, those fighting knights, those hunters winding their horns? Many bodies are there seen under one head, or again, many heads to a single

> body. Here is a four-footed beast with a serpent's tail; there, a fish with a beast's head. Here again the forepart of a horse trails half a goat behind it, or a horned beast bears the hinder quarters of a horse. In short, so many and so marvellous are the varieties of divers shapes on every hand, that we are more tempted to read in the marble than in our books, and to spend the whole day in wondering at these things rather than in meditating the law of God. For God's sake, if men are not ashamed of these follies, why at least do they not shrink from the expense?'

Secular carvings, grotesques, monsters, fertility symbols and profane subjects are as likely to be found in cathedrals and former monastic churches as they are in remote parish churches; indeed such carvings have often survived best among the roof bosses in the high stone vaults of the great churches where they are often scarcely visible from the ground and where they have also been exceedingly difficult to reach by puritan reformers or iconoclasts. The remarkable array of secular subjects, monsters, grotesques, mermaids, strange beasts, acrobats and other curiosities displayed on the roof bosses of the cloisters in the former nunnery at Lacock seem to the twentieth century mind strangely at odds with the contemplative religious life to which the nuns were dedicated. The tradition of such carvings was, however, established very early and persisted throughout the Middle Ages. The best example in the country is in the crypt of Canterbury cathedral where the capitals were carved during the early twelfth century. Here, at the very heart of English Christianity, and in a church whose architecture and decoration had profound influence throughout the country, not one of the carvings on any of the capitals has any religious theme or significance. Instead the subjects chosen by the carvers include fabulous animals playing musical instruments, fighting beasts, monsters, dragons, grotesque creatures and contortionists. It was as though, even in the twelfth century, the Church still felt obliged to cater for the tastes of a basically pagan, imperfectly christianised population, and still emphasised the old pagan demons and pandered to medieval humour and liking for caricature. In the west-country the same thing can be observed at Wells. It was at Wells cathedral early in the thirteenth century that a new and distinctively English style of foliage capital was developed for the transepts and eastern part of the nave. These capitals show for the first time the fully-developed stiff-leaf foliage, deeply-cut naturalistic foliage, a luxuriant pattern of leaves forming one of the most beautiful designs ever produced by stone-carvers. Yet the Wells stiff-leaf capitals have another feature, for the leaves are inhabited by an array of grotesque characters who peer out from the foliage. One capital shows a peasant grimacing apparently with toothache, another has a scaly dragon, others show fighting monsters, devils, a man removing a thorn from his foot, thieves robbing a vineyard and an assortment of fantastic creatures. Stiff-leaf carving similarly inhabited by a weird assortment of grotesque creatures can be seen in the

Elder Lady Chapel at Bristol cathedral which was built only a few years after the Wells capitals, probably during the years 1215-1225. A fragment of a letter survives in which Abbot David who was responsible for the Elder Lady chapel asked the Dean of Wells to send carvers to Bristol to do some of the work, and there is naturally a close similarity in style. As at Wells, the Elder Lady Chapel has superb deeply-cut foliage decoration of very high quality, and, as at Wells, the foliage is full of little figures, a monkey, a goat, a fox and goose, faces peer out, and grotesque biting heads grasp the ends of mouldings. This tradition of high-quality naturalistic foliage decoration continued in the west-country and can be seen to perfection in the roof bosses of Bristol cathedral, where it has been possible to identify at least fifteen different species of leaf in the carvings.

In considering the main secular subjects to be found in stone-carvings throughout the region it will again be convenient to treat each in turn, although it has to be remembered that many churches have a complete jumble of subjects and that secular and religious carvings are often intermixed and are found in juxtapositions which seem strange to the modern eye. A few churches in the region contain re-used Roman material, notably Compton Dando near Keynsham, where a Roman altar stone with fine carvings of two Roman gods, possibly Jupiter and Hercules, is built into the north-east corner of the church: this has now been recognised as part of the great sacrificial altar which stood in the temple of the goddess Sulis Minerva in Bath. At Tockenham between Chippenham and Swindon a sharply-cut Roman figure of Aesculapius is displayed in the south wall of the church; and pieces of Roman figure sculpture are built into the churches at Daglingworth and Churcham in Gloucestershire.

One of the most interesting of all secular carvings to be found in a parish church in the region is at Codford St Peter near Warminster in Wiltshire. This is a narrow panel on a four-foot high stone block which once formed part of a ninth-century Saxon cross shaft. It depicts an elegant male figure with head thrown back, holding a branch of foliage in one hand and executing a stylised dance. The figure is remarkably well carved, with flowing clothes, drapery and beautifully designed shoes, and detail of the pin which holds his cloak. In his left hand the dancer holds a mallet, and there seems little doubt that he represents Sucellos, the mallet god, a powerful fertility figure in pagan mythology. The fact that he appears on a Saxon cross-shaft is an interesting example of the way in which the early Church embraced and incorporated the pagan gods into its own symbolism.

Equally remarkable is the way in which the Church absorbed the pagan beliefs which involved human male and female fertility symbols. Several of these blatantly sexual figures survive on churches in the region, and we can only wonder how such remarkably explicit carvings can have survived the Puritanism of the seventeenth century and Victorian restorations of the nineteenth century, and we can only speculate how many more once existed but have fallen victim to those who regarded them as obscene. Good examples of the female fertility figure known as a 'Sheila-na-Gig', which consists of a grotesque woman with exaggerated sexual organs, are to be found at Oaksey between Malmesbury and Cirencester, at Ampney St Peter near Cirencester, at Fiddington near Bridgwater, and on roof bosses in St Mary Redcliffe and Wells cathedral, and there is a badly weathered example on the south wall of the chancel at Clevedon; blatantly masculine figures, again with exaggerated sexual organs, survive at Abson near Bristol and Haresfield south of Gloucester. The Abson figure in particular is extremely clear and explicit. Carvings of the Green Man, the pre-Christian symbol of vegetative fertility, a figure surrounded by foliage and often with foliage emerging from mouth, nose and ears, are to be found both inside and on the outside of very many churches in the region. He is to be found on roof bosses in St Mary Redcliffe, at Wells cathedral and Lacock Abbey, he peers out from among the stiff-leaf foliage of the Elder Lady Chapel in Bristol cathedral, and is constantly to be found amongst the stone-carving on village churches, and on numerous wooden bench ends. He is even to be found incorporated into specifically Christian carvings, as at East Brent where on the western face of the tower a series of carvings depicting the Trinity and the Blessed Virgin rest firmly on the figure of the Green Man. Again, we can only speculate as to why medieval carvers turned so frequently to this figure as the inspiration for their work throughout the whole of the Middle Ages.

Other subjects portrayed in stone-carving can be dealt with more briefly. Human heads are of course almost universal in medieval carving, and while some represent kings, bishops, monks and actual persons, others, especially the earlier heads, may be a survival of Celtic beliefs about the human head, and the severed head motif which is to be found in Celtic art. The Celtic cult of the human head was taken into the Christian church and the severed head or *tête coupée* is one of the most widespread and characteristic figure carvings in churches. Just as to pagan minds, the severed human head was a powerful force in averting evil, so the decoration of Christian churches returns again and again to the human head, naturalistic or grotesque, in bosses, capitals, windows and doors. Two particularly interesting heads are to be found on either side of the chancel at Orchardleigh near Frome. One is a monk and the other a nun, and each holds a large iron ring. These have an essentially practical purpose, to hold up the lenten veil or cloth which was hung across the chancel during Lent. Similar heads, which were intended to serve the same purpose, can be seen in the chancels at Portbury and Portishead. In the Elder Lady Chapel of Bristol cathedral and in many other places, biting heads can be seen gripping the ends of columns and mouldings, and throughout the region human heads are to be found as 'label stops' or ornamental bosses at the ends of the hood moulds around windows and doors, both inside and outside churches. Most of these heads are either grotesque or are obviously stylised and not intended to represent any particular person. A few however may have been taken from life, although rarely does any evidence survive. A few of the bosses in Bristol cathedral seem as though they may represent actual people, and it has been strongly argued that two corbels on the doorway heads at the east end of the cathedral, one of a young King and the other of a young Queen, must date from c.1330 and are intended to portray the young Edward III who was then eighteen years of age and his Queen Philippa who was a patron of this Augustinian abbey. Many churches have examples of Norman biting heads, fearsome beaks and grinning monsters with large teeth. Examples may be seen at Lullington, Elkstone, Compton Martin and many other places, and the tradition of biting, grinning heads was continued in roof bosses and numerous examples may be seen in St Mary Redcliffe. In the roof bosses here and elsewhere we can also see the motley assortment of motifs which appealed to the medieval carver or to the humour and superstition of medieval congregations, subjects as diverse as mazes, ships, mermaids, foxes, geese, pigs and other birds and animals, jesters, centaurs, and all sorts of strange creatures. Finally in a few places we can find carvings which appear to have no relevance to churches either as decoration or as symbol, and which to the modern mind seem totally unsuitable if not disgusting. There are several examples at St Mary Redcliffe including a roof boss under the tower of a man seated on a privy and holding his nose; two similar figures are found on the roof bosses in Wells cathedral. On the tower at Churchstanton, south of Taunton, a male figure extends his buttocks backwards over the parapet and is used as a water-spout. Such figures can only represent the coarse humour of medieval masons, and are further evidence of the fact that the choice of subject for carvings was very often left entirely to the mason, just as wood-carvers seem to have been allowed absolute licence, especially in carving misericords. We can also find a great variety of odd creatures in the corbels and gargoyles on the outside of churches. Among the monsters, demons, fierce beasts and glaring creatures, we can find examples of the Green Man, the Centaur, the Mermaid, various animals and birds, *anthropopagi* or man-eating monsters. A good example of the latter is to be seen on the south wall of Seend church in Wiltshire; this church also has a man playing on bagpipes. On the north side of the nave at Lacock parish church a lively series of late medieval corbels includes one of a man apparently smoking a pipe; this seems unlikely before the introduction of tobacco and he must presumably be playing a pipe of which a part may perhaps have been broken off.

5 *Destruction of Stone Carvings during the Reformation*

It is important to remember that the surviving carvings both in wood and stone in our churches represent only a small fraction of what they once possessed. Sculptural losses at the time of the Reformation were immense, exceeded only by the losses of mural paintings and stained glass windows. Images of Christ, the Blessed Virgin and the Saints were identified with idolatry and were ruthlessly torn out of churches and smashed leaving only a few survivors and fragments to remind us of what once existed. Fortunately the carvings on roof bosses and high up on towers and parapets were out of reach of all save the most fanatical and enthusiastic iconoclasts. The inventories which survive from immediately before the Reformation for some churches, for example St Ewen, Bristol 1455, or Pilton in Somerset 1509 give some indication of the fine furnishings, colourful carvings, images and other possessions of the churches. The surviving churchwardens' accounts with their records of money spent on the churches also show the profusion of tombs, effigies, images, capitals, carved wall surfaces and exterior statues and carvings which once existed, and the fact that they were all liberally covered with paint and gilding; the accounts also show the extent of the destruction during the religious changes of the sixteenth century. For the twentieth century observer this absence of colour from church interiors and from surviving carvings which have been stripped bare of colour by various restorations, is a great handicap in visualising the interior appearance of an English church or the original appearance of the carvings.

The destruction began with the religious changes of the 1530s. In 1538 Henry VIII issued a series of Royal Injunctions one of which contained a stern warning against the superstitious veneration of statues and relics, and ordered the clergy to caution their congregations against 'that most detestable offence of idolatry' and warn them that

> 'images serve for none other purpose but as to be books of unlearned men that cannot know letters, whereby they might be otherwise admonished of the lives and conversation of them that the said images do represent; which images if they abuse for any other intent than for such remembrances, they commit idolatry in the same to the great danger of their souls . . .'

Immediately some churches began to take down and destroy their images of Christ, the Virgin and the Saints. For example in Bristol the All Saints' account shows that 2d. was paid to the clerk and sexton 'for takyng downe of the Imags'. As throughout the whole of the Reformation period, it was only statues and carvings which might be thought idolatrous which were liable to destruction or defacement, and effigies on tombs, figures of birds, animal or grotesque monsters were regarded as unexceptional and escaped destruction.

Between 1536 and 1540 the monasteries and religious houses of monks passed to the Crown. This was accompanied by a holocaust of destruction, as lead was removed from roofs, buildings were gutted or destroyed and images and carvings cast out. The extent of the destruction can be readily appreciated by a visit to any of the sites of the former great monasteries of the West Country — Glastonbury, Hailes, Malmesbury, Muchelney, Keynsham, Bath, Hinton Charterhouse and a score of others.

A further wave of destruction came with the accession of Edward VI in 1547. Fresh Royal Injunctions ordered the clergy and churchwardens to destroy all shrines and all 'monuments of feigned miracles, pilgrimages, idolatry and superstition and to warn their parishioners against the danger which these things presented to their immortal souls. At Christ Church in Bristol the churchwardens paid 6s. 4d. to six men 'for taking down of the Images at the high aulter', and twenty vats of rubble and broken images were carried out of the church. At St. Ewen in Bristol the statues in the church were all taken down and destroyed. Workmen were paid 10d. for 'takinge downe the tabernacles with the Images' and a further 1s. 4d. for 'takinge downe the Roode and the rest of the Images' while a mason was paid 1s. 6d. for 'dressing upp the walls by the hye Altar' in other words for repairing the scars left by the removal of the statues. Similar examples of demolition can be multiplied from wherever churchwardens' accounts survive to bear witness to the destruction. It required only one determined man in a parish to destroy much of great beauty and value within a church, like one Forde who was a master at Winchester College and who objected to the statues in the College Chapel as being idolatrous. One night, therefore, he

> 'tyed a long coorde to the images, lynkyng them all in one
> coorde, and being in his chamber after midnight, he
> plucked the cordes ende, and at one pulle all the golden
> godes came down with *heyho Rombelo*'.

It is remarkable that the orgy of destruction produced no protest, especially since many of the things destroyed, woodwork, vestments, paintings, statues, were things which the congregation had themselves helped to pay for. But throughout the Bristol area no record of any protest survives. The changes were of course enforced with all the authority of Church and State, and opposition was dangerously linked with treason and with its terrible penalties. Many no doubt conformed for the sake of peace and in hope that the times would eventually change; others of course were sympathetic to reform and saw the destruction of images as a necessary part of that process.

The year 1550 saw the strongest measure of all by the government. This was the Act against Superstitious Books and Images which heralded another period of massive destruction of anything which might be accounted superstitious or idolatrous in stone, wood or glass, though the Act specifically excluded all effigies and statues which had not been reverenced as saints. In Bristol, the St Werburgh's accounts show payments for demolishing the stone altars and the destruction of images and of the great screen surmounted by the Rood which divided the nave from the chancel. The churchyard cross which had an elaborately carved top containing images of the saints was also smashed. Twenty-one loads of stone and rubble were taken out of the church, and the street cleaner (the 'Raker') was paid 8d. 'for carrying away ye Dust'. Later some scandal was caused in Bristol when children were found playing with parts of images and other items which had been cast out from the churches.

Some restoration occurred during the reign of Queen Mary (1553-1558), but upon the accession of Elizabeth in 1558 a further spate of destruction was ordered. The churchwardens' accounts of Christ Church, Bristol, tell their own story:

1558-9

To the ringers at the comyng (i.e. accession) of the Queen	8d.
For puttyng owt the Images at the alter	6.
For takyng down of the Rode and Images	1s. 0d.
For brekyng down of the alters	4s. 0d.
To the Raker for carrying the rubble out of the church	1s 4d.
A mason and his man to make up the walls	2s. 0d.

When the extent and thoroughness of the destruction of these years is considered, and when it is recalled that further horrific destruction of images and of what they regarded as 'the relics of Popery' was carried out by the Puritans in the seventeenth century, and that many Victorian restorations were unnecessarily thorough and destructive of much that was old in the churches, then it is a marvel that so much has survived to enable us to reconstruct in imagination what the churches once looked like and to realise the splendour of the medieval stone carving that once existed.

Index of Churches

Illustrations shown in bold

Saxon Crucifixion or 'Rood' from the church of the Holy Rood at Daglingworth near Cirencester, c. 1050.

Above: *Late Saxon carving of the Virgin and Child from Inglesham in north-east Wiltshire. Note the word 'Maria' above the Virgin's head, the typical Saxon* motif *showing the hand of God dominating the scene, and the large figure of the Christ-child holding a book in his left hand, his right hand raised in blessing. This carving is now inside the church, but the sundial beneath the seated Virgin makes it plain that it was originally outside.* Opposite (top): *The Tree of Life tympanum from Siston, twelfth century. This was a popular theme with Norman carvers, and was associated both with the tree of Man's Fall in the Garden of Eden and with the Cross of his Redemption.* (middle): *Late Norman tympanum showing the* Agnus Dei *from Langport.* (bottom): *Charmingly naive Norman tympanum from Stoke-sub-Hamdon near Yeovil shows the Tree of Life, the Agnus Dei and two signs of the Zodiac, Sagittarius and Leo.*

Opposite (top): *St Michael and the dragon from the tympanum above the north door at Moreton Valence. This is a late twelfth century copy in stone of a manuscript illumination. The winged figure of the archangel Michael is shown thrusting his spear into the mouth of the dragon who rests against a background of foliage.*
(bottom): *Primitive carving of St Michael fighting a dragon from Stoke-sub-Hamdon, early Norman or possibly Saxon.* Above (left): *Part of the elaborately carved Norman font from Southrop near Cirencester. This shows the Virtues triumphing over their contrary Vices. Here Patience (Paciencia) is subduing Wrath (Vra). The names of the Vices are carved in mirror-writing as a further indication of their wickedness.* (right): *The figure of Moses from the Norman font at Southrop near Cirencester. Moses is shown holding the tables of stone, and with two horns; the horns were a convention in medieval depictions of Moses because of the mis-translation of a word in the Vulgate which was mistakenly thought to describe Moses as* cornuta *or 'horned'. Above are the Heavenly Mansions to which Baptism and the other Sacrements of the Church provide admission.*

Left (top): *Elkstone near Cheltenham, the ornate Norman tympanum showing Christ in Majesty surrounded by the symbols of the Evangelists with the hands of God above. Note the fine beak-head ornament on the surrounding arch and the biting head above the arch.* (bottom): *Some of the Apostles from the powerful tympanum at Malmesbury Abbey c. 1155-1165. One of the most important and dramatic examples of Norman sculpture in the country.*

Norman carving from the chancel of the former Augustinian priory of Leonard Stanley near Stroud. This shows the woman who annointed Christ's feet and wiped them with her hair.

The figure of the Risen Christ trampling upon the sleeping soldiers at the Resurrection from the beautiful fifteenth century tower of Ile Abbots.

God the Father with the Crucified Christ, a fifteenth century carving at the apex of the west front of Yatton Church.

Coronation of the Virgin on the west side of the tower at East Brent. The Virgin is crowned by the figure of the Rising Christ holding in his hand the orb of the world.

Fifteenth century figures of the Virgin and Child from the Ham stone tower at Ile Abbots.

(top): *The Risen Christ displaying the wounded hands on a roof boss in St Mary Redcliffe. This is a good example of the fine roof bosses in the high fifteenth century roof of St Mary Redcliffe which are only visible with difficulty from the floor of the church.*
(bottom): *God the Holy Ghost from a roof boss in St Mary Redcliffe. This is one of the three bosses high above the south transept of St Mary Redcliffe; the other two figures are undoubtedly intended to represent God the Father and Christ, and this is presumably intended for the Holy Ghost, but the reason for the figures and grotesques in the hair and beard is a mystery.*
Opposite: *An angel above the ornate fifteenth century porch at Yatton.*

Top: *Grotesque figure from the outside of Banwell Church near Weston-super-Mare.*
Bottom: *Male fertility figure on the east wall of the chancel at Abson near Pucklechurch.*
Opposite: *A man-eating monster from the south wall of Seend Church near Melksham. Such 'anthropophagi' were a popular subject with carvers.*

A grotesque laughing imp or monkey climbing the south wall at Evercreech, the embodiment of mischief and disorder. These Evercreech figures are Victorian but carved in a much earlier tradition.

Norman tympanum from Leonard Stanley near Stroud showing two beasts holding a mutilated human head. This theme of beasts devouring a human head is very ancient and is to be found in pre-Christian Celtic art from all over Europe.

A female figure in Doulting stone from Chesterblade near Shepton Mallet.

Top (left): *A scaly creature apparently devouring another, from the roof of Somerton Church.* right: *A bagpipe player from the wall of the ornate north aisle at Seend near Melksham which was built at the expense of a local clothier, John Stokes, during the late fifteenth century.* Bottom (left): *A gaping monster holding his ears used as a gargoyle at Chewton Mendip.* right: *A late medieval winged monster from the roof parapet at Yatton.*

Another grotesque, grinning monster from Steeple Ashton.
Opposite: *Corbel of a horned and scaly demon from Evercreech.*

A curious figure from the Norman corbel table around the chancel at Stoke-sub-Hamdon near Yeovil. Another example of the fascination of the severed head or tête coupée *for stone carvers.*
Opposite: *A late medieval grotesque beast climbing the parapet at Steeple Ashton.*

Grotesque beast with webbed feet from St Mary Redcliffe.

Opposite (top): *Two life-like figures supporting niches for saints at St Mary Redcliffe.*
(bottom): *Two musicians from the Elder Lady Chapel at Bristol Cathedral. The remarkably varied collection of thirteenth century carvings in this chapel includes monkeys, a goat, a fox and goose, and many grotesques as well as St Michael and the Dragon.*

One of the famous series of carvings from the early thirteenth century capitals in the south transept at Wells Cathedral where a motley collection of secular figures peer down from among the superb stiff leaf foliage.

An acrobat or jester performing remarkable feats of agility on one of the roof bosses in the fifteenth century cloister at Lacock Abbey. The splendid series of carved bosses here includes many secular and pagan subjects.

A musician from High Ham Church near Street in Somerset.

A fifteenth century corbel from Yatton Church which looks as though it could have been carved from life.

The continuing tradition of stone carving. This angel bearing a sickle is from the nineteenth century church at Chantry near Frome which was built by the Fussell family whose fortune was founded upon the manufacture of edge tools such as scythes, sickles and axes.

Figures from the incomparable West Front at Wells Cathedral showing both the fine workmanship and also the effects of seven centuries of exposure to Somerset wind, rain and frost.

Late Saxon relief depicting the 'Harrowing of Hell', from Bristol Cathedral. Note the powerful figure of Christ triumphing over the jaws of Hell, the figures of the saved lifted by the Cross, and the agonised soul in Hell beneath.

Figure from the West Front of Wells Cathedral.

Bibliography

J. Andersen — *The Witch on the Wall,* 1977

M. D. Anderson — *History and Imagery in British Churches,* 1971

J. H. Bettey — *Church and Community: The Parish Church in English Life,* 1979

— *Bristol Parish Churches during the Reformation,* 1979

— *The Landscape of Wessex,* 1980

C. J. P. Cave — *Roof Bosses in Medieval Churches,* 1948

R. W. Dunning — *Christianity in Somerset,* 1976

— *Somerset and Avon,* 1980

A. Gardner — *English Medieval Sculpture,* 1951

B. Little — *The City and County of Bristol,* 1954

N. Pevsner — *The Buildings of England: Somerset, 1958 (2 vols, including Bristol)*

— *The Buildings of England: Wiltshire,* 1963

A. Ross — *Pagan Celtic Britain,* 1967

L. F. Salzman — *Building in England,* 1967

R. Sheridan and A. Ross — *Grotesques and Gargoyles,* 1975

M. Q. Smith — *The Sculptures of the South Porch of Malmesbury Abbey,* 1975

— *The Roof Bosses and Vaults of Bristol Cathedral,* 1979

L. Stone — *Sculpture in Britain during the Middle Ages,* 1955

D. Verey — *The Buildings of England: Gloucestershire,* 1970 (2 vols)